Andy Muse

Those and Me

Andy Muse

Amuse Me Press - 2016

Copyright

Copyright © 2016 by Andy Muse

All rights reserved. This book or any portion thereof may not be reproduced or used in any manner whatsoever without the express written permission of the publisher except for the use of brief quotations in a book review or scholarly journal.

First Printing: 2016

ISBN 978-1-911275-00-8

Amuse Me Press

www.amusemepress.co.uk

Dedication

To those wild nights spent drinking in and burning
with another lovers skin.

Contents

SPRING

The Recovery

One Night

The Mine

Their First Time

In Preparation

Becky

She Laughs

The Jewel of Ullapool

She

From A Train

The Burning

Efamore

New

SUMMER

The Beautiful

She Is Back

Hey Sister! Where Did You Get That Walk?

Lust

Holly Is Laura

Being Her

Drinking

We Love Nice

Up Front

What?

Rowan

Morningness

She's Me

AUTUMN

Discarded

Her Time

I Took Her Advice

Taste

Bricks

Night Out

Fuck Off

Cold

Equals

Where We Should Be

Winter's Fingers

Epic Cunt Rant

Another Dream

WINTER

Turn And Stop

Dream 2

He Saw Her

You Know Why

Time For A Boil Wash

The Storm

Black

Sufjan Stevens

His Birthday

Sacrifice

Hardening

Icicle

Binned

Contact Me!

Andy Muse

Reactions To A First Reading

Preface

This, my first collection, has been in no small part a millstone hanging heavy from a rusting chain about my neck. Perhaps a few of the poems need a little tidying, a few more hours of micro adjusting, but hey, I had to release myself from its clutches and sign off on it.

I had grand designs for this volume. I envisaged it being a coffee table book with photography illustrating each poem, with video telling the tales and with a limited hand crafted edition of multi-media artworks.

The format was to be 52 poems written with relationships in mind and linked to the seasons. So 13 poems per season, the poetry reflecting the accepted associations that have attached themselves to each.

I have laid out the book in this way and there are still 52 poems but I have decided to let the words speak for themselves, wishing to publish now and not in two years time, or, perhaps, never. I will work on photos and publish the images that accompany this book of poetry... Maybe... One day...

I began this collection on a creative writing degree course that I managed to attend for about half a year. The course was useful in helping me to understand the need for correctly laying out my words, to edit and to spell check. However, with regards to creativity and support, it was left wanting. That was in 2010.

Since then, some years I have not written at all and some I have worked erratically, maybe producing a few lines a month. But 2015 saw a change in this and I have worked consistently since September, snatching spare moments and spending evenings editing away, with the end goal to release myself from these poems.

Some are angsty, angry and accusatory while others are melancholic. I do hope you also find comedy in a few of them. They are written with the male in mind. By this I do not mean these poems are for men, but I hope to reflect the male experience of love and relationships and hopefully in stark and memorable lines.

The poems are what I have been or rather how I have felt. They are not me as I am now, not how I feel now. I find that writing sets down the truth (to me), and draws a marker pen thick line under it. I can then walk on without turning back. And so I regard this book as a journal of my self administered therapy.

I also believe this collection to be in part a reflection of an other me, so, a tongue in cheek look at a male perspective of relationship, but written perhaps by a naughty boy. Of course some poems are fantasy and some are recollections of other than me's that I have hijacked and incorporated into these tales. I will leave you to ponder on the veracity or ownership of the content.

In general, the shorter the poem the older it is. The word count has grown alongside my man ears, nose and occasionally, beard.

I follow no forms and although I understand and can write in some I choose to let the rough draft dictate the rhyme and pace and layout. And yes, against the advice of lecturers, most of my poems do use rhyme. After all, a prose poem is still prose, isn't it?

I hope that this allows for interest for the reader. I hope this manages to engage you and encourage you to read on through to the last page. For me that is important as this is a complete book not a collection of disassociated parts. It will take you on a journey from being lost, through gaining confidence and falling in and reveling in love, through crisis and pain only to return to being lost once again.

I have chosen to write in a style that is easily accessible, using few references and lines with hidden meaning. This is important to me and is how I see good writing working for the reader. It's not dumbed down vocabulary. For me, it is heartfelt and understandable.

And now it is done. It is published and you are reading it. This means I can move onto other projects. I have more poetry (coming soon), photography, short stories and a collection of pieces drawn from a Cardiff based writing group that I facilitate. However, next to be published will be a conspiracy fact book which aims to be a guide to truth in the 21st Century. I have the chapter titles and will start writing this early in 2016.

These will all be published by Amuse Me Press and will be available both as digital downloads and printed editions.

At the end of this book of poetry I ask you to contact me with criticism, constructive or otherwise.

Publishing this first collection has been a learning process and I wish that process to continue. I am grateful for any interactions with those who show interest.

Andy Muse

December 2015

Spring

The Recovery

She was snow light;
she shone by his side.
He was coal black.
He was wolf pack.

Her soul was sharp;
she slashed at his senses.
He was icy hearth.
He was fake laugh.

Her shade seeped;
she strode within his storm.
He was ages passed.
He was bull glass.

She shares her shape still;
sensual saviour.
He is fully grown.
He is saved bones.

One Night

I said no
She read maybe.
Her love was slow
to grow on me.

But grow it did
despite her odour,
her fetid breath
her squirming ardour.

She rarely washed
her stinking skin,
that on me squashed,
then I was in.

I said 'yes!'.
She read great passion.
I later dressed
in untimely fashion.

The Mine

I stood naked
that day that wedded
the birthing cries
of hers, of mine.
I, who for a time,
protected her,
she, gentle mother,
straining to best
but from her clay
sculpted breast
she turned away,
slip slipping
and I, enchanted
by this pissing
on the parted,
demanded nothing...

We walked beside
the tumbling roar
then climbed beyond
the cascades claw
to gain a path
ancient and thin
with mighty drops
beckoning falling

till a broader patch
appeared before us
a patch to catch
the moonlit forest
which hid in it's space
a darker dark
a mawr of pitch
the blackest mark.

I gathered Jess near
and she stuck close
as we, within fear
approached our host
the ghost of past
the remains of toil
a portal in time
vomiting spoil
and in we wandered
over rough hewn track
passing pillar, stall
and abandoned slag
to be mothered by
embracing arms
of cold damp stone
of dripping sounds.

Our torches we lit
and we stepped on
exploring the depths
of a place forgotten
it's hacked out arches
and abandoned steel
the winding gear
wire rope and wheels
until lost in thought
and lost in space
with notions of loss
heartbeats raced
we were lost in mind
and time stood still
in the mine shrouded
with visions evil.

We viewed horror scenes
set deep underground
with drowning pools
and creatures found
in labarynth's thrall
who'd drag all down
with one intent
to gouge and maul
but we held our own
and searched the halls
ignoring the groans
and our deathly palls

until an incline we saw
it was the way out
so we groped and pawed
we raced in a rout.

Always upward the trend
on hands and knees
blood oozing from scrams
lungs fighting to breathe
from panic most blind
in the bowels of the earth
in the night black heart
in the belly of her
until at a small crack
an aperture like cunt
Jess and I both
squeezed out as runts
bedraggled and weak
from struggles within
our minds and the mine
we were reborn, feeling

Alive! Alive! Alive!
We had emerged safe
and under the stars
light enough for the brave
we hugged and danced
caring not of danger
as we had survived

the wrath, the anger
of sacred scarred mother
with innards spilled
tortured by others
the ghosts in the hill
and we laughed and whirled
but then was a cracking
a vibration so loud
and Jess lost her footing.

From once great joy
to screaming terror
Jess swallowed whole
all bar her fingers
which lingered on
the lips of the mother
who was gulping her down
with each new tremor.
I held out my hand
for her to grasp
but to little avail
her strength had passed
so I watched her slide
with emotions detached
back into the earth
from where she had hatched.

...and there we have it
Jess is no more

and the wrench from me
by mothers claws
was no great trauma
as now she's home
and I continue on
to shake my bones
in a daily dance
that has no meaning
but does entrance
and implies feeling
so watch me close
as I capture your gaze
with slight of hand
now you're ablaze
that's the magic in me
that you can't see
and you're next in line
for me to free!

Their First Time

She lay on the bed wanting him,
oh, so wanting him.

His tongue stuck to her back,
gently gliding down her spine,
over the soft downy hair,
the warm damp skin,
sliding over the heat of her cunt
as she rolled over and offered herself,
digging at her belly button,
sucking at each breast before
the kiss.
That long, penetrating, discovering kiss.

His lips were glued to her lips as
gently his hand stroked her leg,
over the faded pink birthmark,
the speed line scars,
sliding over the changes in skin
as she parted her legs and offered herself,
digging at her inner thigh,
sucking at her tongue before
the fuck.
That long, adventurous, loving fuck.

And she lay on the bed, wanting him,
oh, so wanting him…

And she started to cry
And she threw him off
And she remembered that time
Those times
When it hadn't been like this
And she told him
And they held each other
And he didn't know what to do.

In Preparation

Breakfast
is what we want.
Off really
that cafes don't open
till 0730.

Waiting...

OPEN!

I watch her
eat eggs.
Scrambled.
Quickly downing
builders tea
in dry mouthed
thirsty gulps
making time
to clean her face
from night
from sex larks
from sweaty marks.

Her greasy smears
are a fine base
to paint on.
She nurtures
ivy and

butterflies
with a flick
of her brush.

She's dressing
her daytime self
with magic.

Becky

Each time we meet
I sniff her shoulder
A safe place to greet her
A safe place to smell

She reminds me of love
Those scents I inhale
Those life saving hugs
I'm scarred of those now

She wants to see me
To know who I am
But what does she see?
I give all that I can

And so for excitement
And to share our night
And so to cement us
And for the moonlight

We stumble drunk, uphill,
To midnight mountain we go
Holding hands still and
Drinking wine while it flows

And we stop at the top
And talk many things
Then tumble and drop,
back homeward, clinging

Homes walls hold me
Scold me and beat me
But with her with me
Of my memories I'm free

And so back to Becky
to the things that we do
or did when carefree, but
now, are we through?

Her hand's always cold
But what of her heart?
Such feet, I'm so old, and
Her ears, where to start?

We cwtch like it's food
And explore the flesh
In delicious mood
Loving each caress

We sometime brush over
breast or belly or bum
A fumble under covers then
The suns dawning comes

Her nails paint my torso
Fingers trace her travels
I shiver and buck so
She stops at my navel

As we are friends, just friends
Sleeping deep, like puppies
Her warm body bends
Mine follows, I'm happy

And no, we don't fuck
And I love her for that
I love my good luck but
I'm sad for this fact

And her friends, Dewi, Ben,
Alyn, Chris and Bowen
She shares this with them
She spreads her love thin

But what's new now
Her face has changed
She's looking at me
Differently

And now a kiss
Mouth juices flowing
Sluice gates open
Tongue flicking, teeth biting.

And I can't stop
My hand going there
From toe tip to crown
Her body she shares

And sucking at nipples
I see her flushed chest
She's panting and mewing
It's no time to rest

She starts as my fingers
Find her hot spot
And I want to dig in
I want the lot

And she relaxes as I
Back off from that space
Just stroking its outer
Eyes fixed on her face

It's all just changed
I've fallen in love
I want her to love me
She gives me a shove

And I don't pressure
I want this to remain
Foreplay forever
She's made me tame

And four hours pass
Of kissing and rubbing
Then we get up
And I leave, heart singing

But she said as I left
This can't happen again
And I try to ignore this
Not wanting her plan

And so we go on
Friends in love
Teasing each other
Nightly sleeping together

And no, we don't fuck
And I love her for that
I love my good luck
But I'm sad for this fact.

She Laughs

Her nose

Unlike any other

Yet perfect, placed ideally

Twitches, deforms

Her eyes

Not saucers

Not full stops, like lasers

Beaming, piercing

Her mouth

Creased edges

Lips damp, swollen pink

Arcing, open

All of her

Shaking

Squealing

Inviting me in.

The Jewel Of Ullapool

I arrived needy,
wanting.
I was thirsty for all,
for all things
glittering.

I had been away
nine days...
And so I showered,
swiftly soaping off
the wilderness.

I ate,
and I drank.
I chatted
to Glasgow women
who were thirsty
for a mountain man,
someone other
than a schemie.

And so the waitress
and the climber
touched.
I remember being drunk

and smashing her head
into the slipway.

She was slightly stunned
and I was shocked.
My arms had slipped.
No, my limbs
had an episode.
No action of mine.

All I wanted
was to smooth her,
not to hurt her.

And she'd been through it
In Glasgow
high up
In the towers
and she knew it.
And she knew
It wasn't meant.

And so we kissed
as the sea kissed our feèt
and we partied

with the others
all of them pissed
the service staff
from Glasgow
there, in Ullapool's
Spring and missed
by the boys and mums
of those glorious slums
now parkland
or some such other
redeveloped for the games
the games we play.
But where is she?
Her home's exploded
a 9/11 scene
and her childhood, dead
a concrete dust
Falling as she must
have,
down...

And we parted
from the others
as the night drew in.
She took my hand
and guided me
to her small box room
and single bed
and she carefully

undressed me
as I nervously
and with little skill
tore at her bra.
No hostel bed for me
that night
but her bed
squashed in
fucking.

The next day she worked
and I worked.
I worked through
my hangover and
sitting drinking coffee
I was spotted
by Connor's mother
a lovely from Achnasheen
visiting postcard beauty
Ullapool,
and by chance
me and she said
'What are you doing here?'
And I chatted a wee while
but she had to move on
and I had somewhere
but I didn't really
and maybe
she didn't

have to
too
and we should have so
enchanted
each other
with our connections
our selfless intentions.

I met the waitress
from Glasgow
for a second night
and we drank
and we licked
and we sucked
and in the morning
I kissed her
as though
she were dying
and I made my way
to Inverness
by ponderous coach
where I bought
a few cans
of McEwan's
and I sat on the bank
of the rivers
shimmering bright
and reflected
through my dead head

on how empty
and how full
Scotland can be
and on how empty
and how full are we
and my tinnies
each one, once full,
emptied.

and I worried
about the waitress
and for that day
entertained the notion
a plan almost
placed In motion
to return to the Jewel
of Ullapool.

And to my lasting regret
although likely
for the best
I left her be
but she continues

time without

inside me.

She

Tall and tanned
she bent forwards
before me.

Adjusting her bag,
unaware her top
was revealing

breasts.

Brown on white.
White on brown.

I could only look
and remember.

I wanted
to have her.

I see her breasts now.

From A Train

Within the razor sharp tangle
of snake pit thick growth
rise vigorous rods with
limbs bursting green
from industrial planter
of breeze block drab walls,
once home for engines growl
and worker's sweat. Shouting,
they're busy with production
of what, who remembers?

And of their dreams?

Long decayed and past.
And passed I have travelled
into shadows from brilliance
hid by black clouds swollen
so mighty and menacing
with falling springtime.
Now tears streak the
glass, soft, warm, plump
and the train rolls onwards
tracking its path through time.

The Burning

When I saw her
her eyes
with that liner
her look
straight back
through mine
it hurt but
I thought that
she'd work out
and we worked some
her stripped first
then me
we found a fit
we liked it
and she writes
she's a writer
and one night
after I held her
we shared words
and wine
and for a time
we rhymed
then it was back
to mine
where I placed

light in her mind
played sound at her
and she tripped.
We lay then
and her eyes
looked through
through my time
and I heard yes
so I mouthed over
that rabbit
that sits behind
her right ear
and gently bit
the skin on
her neck.
She shivered
and gasped
so it took me
and I looked
and finger felt
she was on fire
lava poured from her
and she writhed
as I drank her
and she burst

with power.

She had the power.

But then

when I was doing

she slid forward

and her forehead

closed in on

a candle

flaring flame

catching hair.

And so ablaze

above and below

with the stench

of human burning

foaming about us

her body arcing

her sex sparking

we laughed

like babies

seeing bunnies

popcorning.

Efamore

She'll sing for me
as my light dims and
I'll clutch her close
as the leaving begins
though far from me
her sap will be rising
while my roots shrink
and my bark is silent
for time's between us
and she lives large
so I'll dream her up
and then from afar
from afar in space
and distance in mind
I'll think on her
for one last time...

Efa, never, evermore...

But now time spent
is hard golden coin
showered by emperor
with brutish intent
as there's hot lead
sly mingled within

and past digressions
begin onions peeling
but she, sure self
she doesn't move on
to others more worthy
to those forgotten
as me, bright star
least for a moment
these moments spent
in burning foment...

Efa, never, evermore...

So same as then then
when she as a child
her baby thin living
was scalded by spilling
and sloughed off skin
screamed for soft healing
which left crepe hatches
scar tissue brandings
such random scratches
clear liquid markings
enhancing her beauty
enabling a deepening

empathy for all things
including me, fortunately
for it's Efa I'm needing
I see that so clearly...

Efa, never, evermore...

I see her smiling
which is enchanting
her lips drawn wide
I have to join in
her pronounced chin
the crooked tooth
eyes close looking
and her hair, blue
I see young Efa as
lovers love beloved's
but never will love
as she loves others
and they are of her
where I don't fit
so nevermore, Efa
no more, that's it...

Efa, never, evermore...

So on to my death
my passing through
and the promise made
to the Efa now left
living after my cull
her vitals blooming
I leave her my skull
with precious within
things that I loved
not now clasped close
things she'll love
in place of my ghost
and films she'll make
of me, now I'm dead
a star I'll become
my head in her head...

New

When she,
Holly,
left me,
I was left
bereft
in our loft room.
Wooded walls were
a brown pine tomb
and though calling
from deep slumber,
through the ether,
shaking at her,
only sometimes
did she remember
then we talked.
And I drip dropped
into the pitch pit
and the bloody red
it dribbled big.
I was sick.
But bit by bit
I drifted, on it,
through slow time
and all it grew,
the growing ups,

the crashing downs,
those downs I knew.
They were common.
But those grown ups,
they were few.

Then she walked in
and in her I knew
that this one time,
only this one time,
time, it ran anew.
And we played
a loving long game
of make believe love,
living entwined,
hands clasped tight,
wearing kid gloves.
As we weren't open
though we grasped it,
all that we could,
and that goat skin
was baby thin
not thick enough…
And so paired
with close touch,

both yelling yes,
we two knew
that that yes
that we shared
would one day
be too much.
And so together,
before the parting,
we built a space.
And that place,
a steel shell
lined with wood.
And in it I remain
although I could
chant a can do,
more upbeat refrain.
And I should.
But the bloody
it grows inside me
and I repeat
the meat
of the days
that I spent
when the heat
of Holly
left me.

New refrains though,
they develop good

and we'll see
where that leaves me.
With the wood?
Within the trees?
Surely not again,
with new blood...

Summer

The Beautiful

And mostly
I think on the darkness,
the craven,
the barren.
I think on the bitterness.

And I empty.

But that vase
I sometimes fill
with fragrant roses
and wild stems
with heads blooming,
bursting bold.

And until decay,
as winter threatening,
displays it's rot,
I revel in perfumed
rainbow shards,
generous moments
propping up
the props
populating
this sensual

false spring.

And I am there
In the beautiful,
bathing in a rich
purple light
lightly dappled
by leaves from
the last few elms
which stand away
purposefully distant,
sentinels in time,
a time that is past,
as we all are.

But not now.
But not here.

And I knot
a crown of cornflowers
and buttercups
and sun shaped daisies
and anoint her,
placing upon her head
the bright hues

which shine blue
and golden
and crisp white.
And she smiles
a broad, deep,
open mouthed 'yes',
all the while,
I, observing
the inside
of her upper lip,
her gum, pink and wet.
And then her eyes,
grey-green,
ghostly and girdled
by a circle of paler,
softer fractals.
And she sees me...

A furnace blast
with lumpen force
cleaves my skull
and I spark,
absorbing sun,
soaking in her,
goddess of my emptiness.
She places her fingers
into the grey
and she grips,
squeezing electric,
being shocked
by the tales
sketched
in virulent palette
that trickle worm
into her
and out of her lips.

And I grasp her hair
gently tugging it
pulling her nearer.
I'm fishing.
But there's no need
to reel in.
She's definitely hooked
and she's swimming.

And above us
in the high branches
of the bedrock elm
the rooks are home,
observing our rituals,
hearkening to our
squawks, purrs and barks.
And I'm loving them
with their flapping,
squabbling and nesting.
As I am,
ours.

The rooks,
Can teach us a thing
and almost...
I can almost hear,
hear rookspeak.
And the voice
I think,
I think the rooks
repeating cry
Says

'Keep her!'
'Hold her!'
'Love her!'

'Keep her!'
'Hold her!'
'Love her!'

'Keep her!'
'Hold her!'
'Love her!'

And the sun shines.
It shines royally
on us,
on this snatched at day
And I feel it,

I feel the heat
and I know
she's feeling it too.
Somewhere...
Sometimes...
And when I'm filled,
the beautiful,
it's as real as the real
And I ask you
'Why insist the everyday
is more than the ethereal?'
Perhaps your logic
and method scientific
emboldens you...
Those I discarded
some time ago,
so as to witness
and to reach out to
my beautiful ghosts.
And I'd rather be
beside the great elms,
in the beautiful,
in purple,
than walking with you
on those mean and trite
grey skied grey days
as we march
unwittingly
into the terrors.

The beautiful is dutiful,

she glows in my bones.

I am her home.

She paints hot,

she papers me bright.

And when I am taken

and stretched across

the infinite black

she will burst forth

from my fractures

and she will

set you ablaze.

She Is Back

She is back

Her face

Against mine

Her back

Away

She is laughing

And we are talking

About this

And that

How stupid we were

How wonderful we are

Together

We are living

Once more

Making plans

It's been

A dangerous

Time

Hey Sister! Where Did You Get That Walk?

Women
seriously
I build them.

They won't
like that
what I said
but I do.

Women
I build them.

I hold them
when they're
feeling crazy
I shelter them
when the rain
pours in
I take them
to places
imagined,
filling memory,
so that we
might have
seeding.

And I watch
them bloom.

And when
they've rooted
in me
they pluck
at their base
scratch at
my mud
until released
transplanted
they suck up
new foods.

And while walking
the walk
of their own
that was mine
the walk
that I gave them
they sup
the last of me
then keep on
moving

leaving me
searching
for the lost
and for me.

Women
they seem
to love
for a time,
they love
then move on.

Women
seriously
I build them.

Then they love
and move on.

Lust

I'm just there,
higher,
like standing.

I view lands
fertile
and balming.

I watch waves
arcing
and breaking.

And I sway,
shudder,
with feeling.

As I grin,
laughing.
She's inviting.

With arms wide,
reaching,
I'm moving.

Close in now,
clearly
I'm shaking.

And I see
purple
streams pulsing.

So life rich,
surging
with giving.

And the pools,
ovals,
they're brimming.

And I'm so
running,
and bounding.

She's not bound,
restrained.
She's freeing.

There I go,
today,
I'm diving,

straight for the
fertile
moist giving,

and the vales
vibrant
and singing

rise to mounds,
mountains,
she's blooming

with pinnacles
to climb on,
with bumps
to lie down on.

Now she moves,
there,
a rippling.

And she squeals,
tremors,
from tearing

at the mud,
at the blood,
of her.

Holly Is Laura

Back in the day
those days
when I was broken
I found someone
newly mended
and so I pretended
I tried to be strong
and my song
I silently sang.

She lived in Wimbledon
and had been held
a ward on a ward
she wasn't willing
and finding her
for me
changed everything
and she fed me
and I wove words
from the feeding
into my lyrics.

And we lived
and we loved
for three years

and a bit
until one day
a day I never dreamt
though I dream her still
she moved away.

Her moving moved me
more than any other she
and I crashed
and I fractured
into so many he's
that I grew grey
as I gathered
them to me.

I glued the he's
into a new grey me
who was much the same
as the old blondie
but with essence reduced
with energy sapped
and liable to cracking
but once again intact.

Ten years on

and, guess what?
I meet a woman
not yet mended
living in Wimbledon
a ward on a ward
and I am back
breaking myself
digging my flesh
and my song
it's silent
it's had it's best.

Now, come on
what's that about?
The universe and me?
A cosmic shout?

And so Holly
she's become Laura
and in my folly
I want more of her.

Being Her

She said

that when looking at her

He was searching,

searching for himself.

Using her face

as a mirror,

wanting her

to be him.

And she

searched his skin,

bloodshot eyes,

wrinkles, spot.

Did she see herself?

She did?

I think not.

Drinking

She said

that the best time to drink it was morning.

When it is good and strong.

      Concentrated

She said

that I should not leave it long before drinking.

Best to down it there and then.

      Warm

She said

that it was crammed with well-being and stuff.

It would enhance my health.

      Golden

I said

that the following morning I would go for it.

I'm all about trying new things.

      Fluid

I said

each morning I try but each morning I fail.

I awake and strain and watch.

      Showers

I said

it streams to my face and misses my mouth.

It drenches me and my bedding.

      Bonehead

She said

you mean you have not been using a glass?

Man you are just too weird.

We Love Nice

It's nice,

isn't it?

Love and that.

But that love

that we have,

that you have,

it's not right

is it…

As I am me

and you are you

but when we talk

we say we…

Welike

Welove

Wewant

We…

And so where am I?

And where are you?

Am I me?

Are we two?

Or am I you?

Up Front

She told him
she was eighteen.
From Poland.
And she smiled
and stroked him.

He kissed her
dribbling tongue
on cheek,
on neck,
on breast.

And she responded
calmly.
She smiled
then sucked
then shagged him.

He dreamed
'She's my girlfriend'
until it was time,
time to go.
Time's up.

She told him
she was eighteen.
She wasn't.
He'd had to pay,
up-front.

What?

What would you do
If you noticed someone like you
At the edge of your vision
Hacking away at your senses
Delivering hammer blows
At all that you know?

Imagine the familiar
Maybe another
A second you
Tearing at the cloth
Upon which is written
In loving fashion
Your story
As a play of passion.

What would you do
If no matter when,
It could be day or night,
You could be working
Or sleeping
Or just doing nothing,
He or she
Is there?

The other you
Scratching at your eyeballs
Picking at your nose
Pushing clay into your ears
Chatting with you
Well, at...

I think
We all have
Another me
Inside
Checking us
Keeping us in check.

And the brutality
The axing away
For me
Comes from me
Not him.
I think I tell him what to say
But like all thought
I don't know
It could come from you.

And he stays
Never going away
And he says all
That I am to do.

What about you?
Are you you?
Or do you have the other
Talking you through
All that you do?

And no deep cut
Removes him
No drunken night
Has him loosing his way
In the morning
He's there
Proding and poking
Beside and inside.

Rowan

My canine companion, Rowan
is a lurcher fast and golden.
She's oh so attractive to all
well trained, she answers my call.

Her waking life is beside me,
be it mountain, river or sea
with many lazy days of rest,
feotal, she lies on her bed.

When walking and taking the air
unknowingly beauty she shares
with other doggy characters
who pet, admire and chatter.

It's then that thoughts of her master
from her tiny brain flee faster
than she runs and her mind is set
on the attention she gets.

This compels me to smile and chat
to engage, talk doggy and cat
strange stories of four legged friends
micro tales through furry lens.

Stranger's hearts paw towards me,
speaking scenes I don't want to see
painful events and happy too,
but not what I'm here to do.

I want to be walking my pet
in thought as she darts past my legs
but now am burdened by others
Rain, Rowan, head for cover.

Morningness

It is with butterfly eyes, straining against salt-rock blocks glueing wings tight shut, that I glimpse the blisteringly blissful reposing form of my lover. It has been three months and is sumptious summer and I shake myself awake as the sun's shimmer, just a morning's glimmer through glass, feather tickles her nose.

Black snakes lay tangled behind her, trailing serpentine, mimicking night times writhing and coiling. Her lips are partly parted, the opening defined by plump, pink, damp, hotness, hotly inviting me in. And her eyes, stuck fast also, but with the gunge of an Egyptian punk. That liner funk swells my desire for her, it devines her.

I am spying upon the eternal, a pharonic relief I believe, etched in limestone and time stretched by Luxor's sands. Or maybe a carved marble marvel unearthed from Delphic soil, a beauty lost to man but found again. Yet she breathes. And time weighs on her as she holds tight the sights, sounds and tastes of years.

And it is clear, as she twitch turns herself from slumber, I am bewitched. Her spell sticks fast. At last I am anchored in deep waters, deeply in love with love that she authors. I read on her skin solar bright tales of our future living. I watch her until my stirring stirs her and she opens her eyes, smiles and I reverently kiss her.

She's Me

She's a cold fish
a flat bread
she's food to eat
but tasteless.

She's a lovely
with ragged history
unrisen flesh
fractured memories.

She's built a castle
loaves as masonry
wears chainmail scales
conceals her story.

And she's fishing
from her ramparts
she's seeking friendship
for her frozen heart.

But I catch first
I hook her lip
wind in with kisses
she's now on my ship.

And I cherish her
and our time spent
I feast on her
with good intent.

And her fish flesh
well that's the meat
placed within her bread
sandwiches to eat.

And as I consume
all that she is
the walls and scales
well, they aren't missed.

And she starts to warm
to rise and to taste
she proves she can swim
grows strong, with haste.

Now together we walk
as full as can be
full of life's hope
for futures history.

Autumn

Discarded

My pencil penned poems
I've torn into flakes,
now a tattered jigsaw
scattered by my
gently opening palm.

Those musings.
My emotions.
That descriptive
prose passage.
And oh, the rhyme...

Time bound spindrift,
floor bound ghosts.
Each raggedy piece
soulfully falls.
Tearful.

Listen hard.
Can you hear
them yowling
as they flurry
and anoint my feet.
They're greeted there,
as they hurry

to the ground,
hugged there
by the mud,
stuck fast.

There's nothing.
My snow light
insights,
my voice,
it's lost.

What's this though?
Children coming!
Walking my way!

They say words
at each other
those sisters
and those brothers
and not seeing me
they foot stomp
and candy crush
and puddle drench
my heart.

Her Time

The clock stopped
at 12.17
the time when she
invited me
to see her vision
of scenes that she
wanted me
to be painted on
but not in.

But I wasn't
OK with that
and in that man way
that's strong but says
hold on
I think you're wrong
lets hug some
I stood tall
and then didn't
and I begged.

But she was strong
ger than me
and she knew
where she

wanted to be
and that flesh muddle
it was weak
a pretend cuddle
no relation
of how were we
week after week
before our love
curdled,

And is that what I am?
A sour taste man?
Spat out?
To be spat out
never ingested and
made to be the food
that feeds the body
of the one
that if she so wanted
could have eaten
all of me?

And so why bother
with the thought
that one day

the one days past

could once again

be one day?

As it cannot.

And the cannot

is the pain

no matter what

transpires today

and each day

becomes

day on day

for lovers

for ex lovers

throw away.

I Took Her Advice

Vocalise your anger

she said.

It's not good

to hold it within.

Display your emotions

she said.

Don't be afraid

to show feelings.

So I did.

And she left.

Taste

'You are so bitter'
You said

No, you are!
I know this

You taste metallic
That's not right

That first kiss
You were wrong

And now there
Damp and hair

Metallic and flesh
They don't go

You android you.

Bricks

It's the house,

you see,

it holds me.

It was ours.

Not now.

Not now.

We built it

with love,

once enough.

But now alone,

I'm walled in,

and I'm falling.

It was our house

you see,

and it holds me.

Night Out

A friend, Amy, invited me,
she confirmed availability,
prompted and poked me,
so I decided to go.

Roused from my lethargy
I bathed long and vigorously,
well used my perfumery
I was off to a show.

I drove south to the city
the seat empty beside me,
prompting such melancholy,
I still missed her so.

The parking was easy,
Then I walked so slowly,
and stopping momentarily,
my hand held her ghost's.

Then, facing her gingerly
I pleaded for honesty,
wind whistled back bleakly
her voice was as frost.

Shivers ran through me,
my heartbeat thumped wildly
then acting most consciously
I turned and walked fast.

Now striding boldly
the doors parted smoothly
and people looked happy
but where was my host?

My arrival was early,
to the bar for coffee,
I people watched furtively,
inside I was lost

in a world so lonely
without my love Holly
our dreams so destructively
from our doorstep cast.

We once lived so cosily
she wrapped around me,
still where was Amy?
Now rise up the past.

Time flowed creatively
I succumbed to a reverie
of such exquisite beauty
she was with me at last.

Sat laughing beside me
she gazed at me, lovingly,
but I turned, momentarily,
and away she had passed.

Standing quite suddenly
a panic had stricken me,
as maybe she unknowingly
would attend the show too!

With great sense of urgency
lest Amy espied me
I escaped through the lobby
from not one, but two.

Mechanically I quickly
drove off through the city,
homeward so speedily
my friend never knew

of my fleeing so hastily
before she had met me,
after she so kindly
tried to see through

the void glued within me
where she, lost love Holly
resided so perfectly
just one year ago.

How lovers claws lingeringly
clutch so persistently,
their shades so abidingly
cling fast to our souls.

Still fear stalks so starkly,
waiting so patiently,
for she'll meet me eventually
and what then will I do?

Fuck Off

Stop knocking my door.
I know, you know
I'm in.

Can't you understand,
I'm out.

There it goes again
brass on brass.
Your brassy.
I'll grant you that.

Can't you understand.
I'm... Stop knocking my door!
You know, I know
your out.

Cold

It's cold
Cold hearth
Stone cold
Cold heart

Once hot
Hot head
Red hot
Hot bed

Equals

What Is the point
in anything?

I have tried
but I do not
understand
and I think
and think on
but the thinking
realises no
reasonable solution.

And how could it?

I do not have the data
and so my sums
they are failures,
before even
I have marked
an equals onto paper...

Where We Should Be

I never took you
to the places
that I wanted
to show you.

Time moved away
and another day
a second chance
has never been.

I now go alone
to the us spaces
while you're at home
with new faces.

I never took you
to the places
that I wanted
to show you.

And those places
are just spaces
not a warm home
for our faces.

Winters Fingers

Decay caresses our senses, wildly flirting,
dripping brown from wilted stems as growth stalls.
The last blooms are fading,
leaves are blankets falling,
and countrywide
we shudder as winter calls.

For now death stalks the hedgerows,
his scythe hacks at confused sparks there found,
he leaves the fallen to lie,
there awaiting the crows,
yet beauty is met,
if our gaze shifts from the ground.

The reds and browns backlit by a jelly orb,
or the fine morning dew making the visible clear
jewels glistening
on the finest of cords
as the hunter gathers
the last morsels this year.

And the smell, crisp with notes of winter's bark,
a smell to be savoured as soon to be lost,
notes of dying alone
in the dank and the dark,
lost first to the rains
and then to the frosts.

Those crisp frosts that spur the child within
to stamp on glass, paper thin shards strewn,
to step out onto grass,
on it's glistening skin,
leaving footprints as once
men did on the moon.

We plan the perfect Christmas that can never be,
and contemplate a new life come January
when from winter's clutch we will soon be free
but we fool ourselves, if by differing degrees
at work winters effect on our wits I see
for the hardest months are yet to be...

Epic Cunt Rant

I heard a standard voice
Articulating amazement
At our honourable leaders choice
To pluck the leaves of parliament
From the plane trees
One by one by one
Now they are plain
The trees
And our fat controllers
Are controlling natures order
No seasonal splendour
No browns, reds, or yellows,
No fun kicking through piles
Just a barren square
Fitting for a square
And barren state.

Please let them fall
In their own time
A display autumnal
Naturally timeworn
In their own time
Please let them fall.

And I thought

Last straw
Although that aged door
I had wandered to
Some long time before
And my hand had
Pushed open
For me to step through
Some time
In my own time
As I had already seen
All eyes gleaming
Or streaming
You take your pick
And anyway
I might as well
Tell you
You all
Make me sick.
Sick with a rising bile
Boiling up
Through the fracture in me,
The tear that opened
That day
When mum slapped me.
I could take it from him

It's what he did

On occasion

But her?

For repeating a cousins

Naughty rhyme

Not mine...

'Horsey, horsey, please go fast,

If you don't I'll kick you up the arse'.

And oh, my cousins

The troubles they have

Been birthing

And even now

Continue

To spin in

Willfully guided by

Their matriarchal

Other than a mother

She an obscene

'Easterners Pat'

Cockney caricature

Carved in cursed flesh

But dried out

A poisonous lover

Of her brood

Born as food

For her leud

'Carry On' living.

You got all that?

But what you might ask

If so far you have travelled

What is the meaning

Of these lines?

A place to sound off?

A place to lay to rest

The ghosts of one life?

NO!

This poem it's

A call to action

A plea to all

In this nation

And oh so

Farther afield

To make a pledge

Which we must seal

When we sit

And sort

The sickness

That supporates

Within us.

So, I shall tell my story

Illustrating my assertion

That you and yours

All heads need rinsing.

I have a feeling that
The mummified personage
Of my aunt in her dotage
Would deny her feeling
Of me
When a child
I have no memory
Just that feeling
And a knowledge
Of her offspring
Sprung into wrongdoing
Sprung into bed
With whoever
Their hands searching
Tracing images on backs
Gaining confidences
In order to move on
To bum crack.

But I am ahead
Of myself
I wanted to shed
All that was said
And done
As you and I
And others
Placed that boy
On a shelf
Ornamental brother

Dusty now
To be visited
But never
Jumping down.

And so I start
A youthful memory
A blonde four year old me
Somehow feeling sexy
When changing
After swimming
With those teaching
Watching me.

Can that be true?
And if so
It came from who?

Let's move on
And leave that question
To be answered by
My sexualisation
By that aboration
Aunt
Or
Cunt.

And so on to
My neighbours

Russell And Francis
Bending me over
I searching for
The ever elusive
Four leafed clover
Pants pulled down
slapping bum
I think I was seven.

At eleven
With Simon and Terry
Camped out
In the caravan
At the end of the garden

Erection!
Erection!
Erection!

And what to do?
Well nothing for it
But to commando crawl
Down our suburban street.

My first sex thing
Was solitary
Was a surprise!
A waking wet dream
And I came on the sheets

A falling out of bed scene
The gift of a scream
I was relieved and joyful
But I was scared too.

I've masturbated
Most days since
Well, not quite true
As there have been days
When I deliberated
Those days becoming
Orgasm constipated
But I've made up
For lost wank days
On others
Or, with lovers.

And that's how it should be
Exploration of the unknown
Alone, before tentatively
Moving onto sharing
With a peer
Months of touching
As I did with Claire,
Before even thinking
Of penetrating.
I pity you who
Have as a teen
Had sex with an abuser

Who made use of you
Pretended to know you
But urgently moved on
To the next conquest
To a new flesh-fest.

And in case you think
This is a confessional
That's not my thing
That, for me, is unusual
This is so about you
And your sacrificed heart
And all that you see
Of all of life's parts
And so now to the meat
And to the veg too
As I want you to meet
With others, and soon...

At age fifteen
I went to work
For B.T.
My father's dream
Not mine. You see
My hands were tied
As he was fixated
By the need for all
To be urgently animated
By a soulless

(I couldn't care less)
Nine to five
And had I not complied
It was made clear
That my boys life
Would be shaken
And I would drop
From their canopy
Fall from their tree
And be left, not free
But forsaken.

And I worked for a year
In an office
With three women
And I'll fill you in
On the seedier side
Of mother-kind
But first how's about
A fifteen years me
Being asked
To work in
Short shorts
Holding signs
For some sport
-ing event
Wrestling of sorts
Just putting it out there
As an old man did

To me

At Waterloo Station

He expecting elation

From me

At the offer of cash

To display my boy body.

Or he who asked me

What I did at weekends

'Well, I go camping with friends'

'Oh, you like *camping*, do you?'

He was trawling for boy

Wishing for a new toy.

Or Jill

Sat on a train

It was in the station

About to move on

As the carriage door opened

And a man

Pulled away her skirt

And touched her cunt

Just as her doctor

Had.

And so to June,

Not the month

But my BT boss

And to Lorna

And to Yvonne

And to the others...

We drank a lot

At lunchtime

Or at office parties

And Marion

Drunken wife of someone

Went for my cock

And undid my trousers

And touched it

While the others

Watched.

And Eve, she chased me

Round the office

And when caught

Rubbed her breasts

Into my head

Her body

Against mine

Pushing her cunt

Onto my child's hand.

And at Christmas

The telephonists

Lap sitting, on me

Pursuing vocal arousal

My screaming boy cock.

And then it all changed
For I didn't think
This was wrong
Or was abuse
But it's doing
Was not letting loose
Of me, the muse.

And when Karen
Was raped and
Battered to death
I knew I was
Closer to all things
Life stopped
Briefly
And stutters on
Now.
I would have killed him
And still would
If I could find him
But time is ticking
And I never could
Find where he's living.

All of us are predators
Sucking on
The worn nipple
Of the innocent.
Understand that.

Although I'm told we're not.
Predators that is.
At least not all of us.
View you
With honesty...

Are you?

And there were many men
Chancing their arm
Like the man who tried
To undress me
In a busy
Sun filled
Suburban park.
I ran, he ran.

Or the... but...

It's the women that
I remember most
For their innocence
Perfume contrived
Is worn as a cloak
And their ghosts
Have filled my life
Like she who
Groped my bum
At a Forest Hillbillies gig

In the Green man
In Downham.
Like the Scots girls
Who threw themselves
At me
Literally
On a roof
In Paris.
I was drunk
And wanted wine
Not time
Spent kissing
Strangers.

But I'm thinking on
The respected female kind
The pram pushers
The lovely mothers
We should investigate these
As they're lovers
Of more than their
Baby and their mate
And unlike the raincoats
The awkward lone male
The 'He kept himself to himself'
They are not fearful
Of their seeing children
Being mistaken
For mental abduction

And yet their thoughts
They bury deep
As we slumber on
In baby sleep
Through the darkest marks
That they scratch
Held close to chest
Those scenes they hatch
They've lied to us
Me and you
They clothe themselves
In feminine virtue.

So
It's the mothers
The aunts
The grand-mothers
That have flirted
And lusted
And inappropriately
Brushed against me
That bother me most
It's this host
Of womankind
Whose innermost workings
Are the same human feelings
As that of their men
Yet we keep this
Sheltered and hidden.

And I hear their cries
Of self righteous enmity
Against Ovendon
Who wrapt in hubris
Defended himself
With ancient eye
A 'State of Grace'
Was his to find
And to embellish
With painters brush
And a step too far
He may have trod
Not letting them fall
In their own time
But then those women
Claiming moral authority
Who did they crush?
And so now I see
With adult eye
Their faces flushed
And I hear their cries
For what they are...
Transference.

Oh how I've rambled
And bimbled on
And well done
If here you have gotten
But I must draw to a close

This epic of mine
And so back to
Cunt
Or
Aunt.

You see
I've no idea if she
Fiddled with me
But it would answer
Some questions
And help me see clearly
Some actions
And behaviours
That are hard set
Within me
And if she didn't
So what?
She's my icon
For those that
Got their groove on
On my cock.

So, a debate
We must have
To secure our future
Or for those souls
Who come after
For we are done

And need repairing...
Please think on
What all ought
To be sharing.

Please let them fall
In their own time
A display autumnal
Naturally timeworn
In their own time
Please let them fall.

Another Dream

I've not dreamt her
maybe for four years
the four shared years
with the other her.

But the other's past
and she's back
she's at my back
she's back at last.

She paints up lies
her thought crimes
at sleep time
daubed on closed eyes.

How is it that she...
She's still inside me?

And she's back
with a surname change
Rend or Rench.
Remembering names
from within the almost
well, I almost didn't
you know, remember

but I did
and both are suitable
subconscious play
perhaps
or psychic note.

I find myself drawn.
A fierce animal tug
and I am impotent
and I am silent.

She's counting votes
and someone has won
by one
and she has to explain
about a recount
which she does
with BBC'ness
that commonwealth
correctness
and as she holds
the eyes
of all present
in her soft
heart stopping hand

rolling them like marbles
like Chinese balls
I find myself
frozen
not knowing if
she has seen me
and so
I'm floor bound
and shrinking away.

She's a radio show host
has to be in for
a 5am broadcast
one letter and her advice
delivered by her
open mouth
to an awakening.
She is close to being
the voice of god.

How did she get that?
The god thing.
The radio being.

And she has a fair few
acting gigs,
small parts but
It's a start and
who knows where

she'll end up.
She does.
She always has.

I saw her being filmed
in a taxi
for something
maybe 'Eastenders'
and she looks divine
I don't mean wow
I mean radiant
from within, her
translucent skin
displaying the power
of ultra cool
and I have love
for her
and envy of the others
those who now feed her
feed on her.

She's made it
she's almost famous
and after all
she did want to so be
the most attractive
the most desired
and she's there.

The car drives past me

and I can see her smiling

at the man sat next to her

she hasn't seen me

she never sees me now

I am a ghost

fading fast

a shadow in time

a few minutes

to midnight.

For her

I am... I am...

Tick tock.

Tick tock.

I am not.

Winter

Turn And Stop

There had been no debate.
He knew
nothing.

Life must stop for him,
her friend,
her companion.

For I love you no more
she said,
she firmly said.

And I am leaving tonight
she said,
This is right.

But he cannot see the right
in her,
in her leaving.

And he begs her to stay,
please stay,
stay, please stay.

But her mind has turned,
she's turned,
head turned away.

Dream 2

I dreamt her.
We talked.

She said 'I have to go'
but I asked her to stay.
She walked to her mother
who was outside a shop
and she winked at me.

She rejoined me, smiling,
with a pram
and inside, wrapped,
was our baby.

Maybe hand sized, sleeping,
long limbed
like a doll.
I never knew.

And I held him
and dropped him
and he writhed
as an injured cat
writhes. I whirled.
But all was OK.

She gathered him up.

And I spoke to her about him.
The other him.
I said 'I want to hit him'
and she laughed.

She asked me if I wanted
to go to a wedding
of mutual friends
with her
and him
and him.

She wasn't warm.
She was as she was
when she left.

And I woke.
And I want her.
And I don't.

He Saw Her

Whenever he journeys
he looks for her car,
white and small.

Maybe she has sold it.

There are many
small white cars.

Only one of her.

He thinks that she may
have moved away,
somewhere distant.

She has moved on.

There are many
places she can go.

She is distant.

It has been two years
since they met,
for coffee and tears.

He remembers still.

There are many
touching memories.

He is where he was.

There, he sees a car,
it's small and white,
driving past fast.

Can it be her? Is it?

There are many
small white cars.

This car is hers.

And as she passes him
she double takes.
She has noticed.

He is rigid at the kerb.

There are many
places she can go.

She parks nearby.

He crosses the road,
his heart is pounding.
He wants something.

All he wants is her.

There are many
Strong feelings.

He walks to his car.

He turns the key,
turns off the radio
and she is walking,

from her car to his.

There are many
things to say.

Will he ever say them?

He is thinking words
to say to her
as he pulls forward

and their paths cross.

There are many
places they could meet.

They are meeting now.

She says 'Hi' and
'what are you doing here?'
and his voice cracks,

His language scrambles

There are many
words to choose from.

He is lost in his car.

He says 'I'm sorry' and
'I have to go.'
and he drives off

watching her grow small.

He has had many
fucked interactions.

His face is wet.

You Know Why

All know I've left you

And you know why

I know it's my fault

That now you cry

When once

When in love

with emotions so high

And each of us caught

In those slow crafted lies

We danced with the stars

And enchanted ourselves

And running from bars

In deep drunken spells

We fell into our arms

Limbs linked as a cradle

Cocooning each other

Spooning lovers forever

And all know I've left you

And you know why

Our lies are now open

But love lingers... sigh...

Time For A Boil Wash

Let me take you back.

Remember?

I was a clean
crisp
bright
sheet.

I was hanging
on a line
singing
sunshine
with the breeze.

I was thinking
what ought I
in future-times
be.

I would maybe
be the cloth
that covered lovers
as they sweated
and sticky grasped

each others
melting parts.

Perhaps I would
one day become
the preferred shirt
of a lyrical poet
or the garment
loved by a beloved
and treasured long after
they'd loved
and moved on
the lost lover
seeking solace
from the odour
left In me.

I saw me
being dyed purple
become master
of the infinite
a benign ruler of fabrics
the cloth of time.

And for a time

I was treasured   in the dark.

but cleaning

left scars

and each day's efforts

left stretch marks

and despite my service

my protection from sharps

my warmth in cold

my comfort on harsh

as I grew thin

in places

and demanded patches

as stains bloomed

betrayal hatched in faces

and upon my thinning skin.

I'm now folded

hastily

and sit patiently

at the bottom

of a pile

of others.

And I grow mould

my unwelcome spawn

in my creases

and I'm crushed

and so alone.

The Storm

From limestone arch of Roman's hand
the spectacle of fulsome swell churns dark.
Treacle thick, so Mercury fast
and such a tempting place to lie.

With heavens black from rain-clouds swirl
the mighty storm shocks and cracks.
Hammer blows, so daylight bright
and such a perfect time to cry.

From minds cascade with eddies rich
the vivid spectre of beloved rise.
A baby, a mother, a lover drift past,
such tormented visions to hide.

With shattered nights vitality coaxing
thoughts electric surge serene.
Jump now, toward the Siren's light
and such a tranquil place to die.

Black

It seems to me
that despite the sun
washing golden over
the purple shimmer
of Exmoor reclining
lazily above the
green and silver sea,
that all
is
black.

Sufjan Stevens

I love you now

when you visit
for tiny tall tales
and paisley sights,
as time is inhaled,
as I inhale night.

But...

Do you know
what you did
when you said
while sat
at the desk that
I bought you,
in the room
of your own
that I gave you?
"Listen to this"
and you shared
Sufjan with me.

What were you thinking
when you were looking

at my wide eyes smiling
as Sufjan softly sang
his songs of Illinois?

What I was thinking
when being drawn in
by your pupils dilating
was that I loved you
and I loved Sufjan too.

And...

What were you thinking
as our time tiptoed by
and your desk moved
and my days were spent
pacing in your ex room?

What I was thinking
was that as you shared
you were touching him
and so as you shared
he was touching me.

So why did you

when playing
with the new,
why did you
have me be
part of your start
with the new he?
You were strong
and audacious but
you were wrong
to share his share
with you with me.

But...

Sufjan still sings
his songs where
you once sang
fast, happy folk
twisting tongue

but now you don't.

His Birthday

East Lane selling tat,
pie and mash swimming
with eel liquor,
Bermondsey bustling.

And to the pub
for bitter and Guiness,
glass following glass
fueling seething chatter.

It's his eightieth
and I am forty
and he throws out love
then snatches it back.

My brother-in-law, he says,
has a proper job
has done well for himself
and for Ali and the kids.

Why don't I grow up,
put in a good days work.
He doesn't know
that Rob's fucking another.

Then the final cut.
One short sentence.
She was too good for you,
Andrew

I stand tall
with half a lifetime's rage
and I smash my glass
into his face.

For just a moment
I'm astride the globe.
A man, free at last
from him.

But I catch myself.
I slowly stand up
and I say
another pint then?

Sacrifice

I tied her to the kitchen table, I bound
her legs and arms, her wrists and thighs.
I gagged her mouth, taped over her eyes.

I watched her lying stretched and prone.
She was my star, my heart, my flower.
I told her this for a fair few hours.

My words I spat at her closed eyes.
They crashed like pennies falling on stone.
She wet herself, gave a muffled moan.

I stroked her cheek and proceeded on.
Unbuttoned her blouse to see her breast.
Her ribbed and white and heaving chest.

Then I took the sharpest paring knife,
cut through her skin, then began peeling.
I removed her ribs as she was screaming.

Till there it was - her loving part.
Her heart that beat for me in rations,
pulsating wildly, so full of passion.

I reached in, gripped it with both hands.
Her healthy throb stalled then fluttered.
Now she's all mine, to myself, I muttered.

Did I truly rip her life from her?
Of course I did and I will do more.
For she is mine and I am hardcore.

Hardening

She steps up our path no more
But I hear kitten heals on slates
Laid as sediments of sentiment
Ash from the fire of our passion
Now a compressed folio of love

She walks in our home no more
Her key she has returned to me
And it turns on me in my pocket
Pricks flesh with barbs she spat
Sticking sharp in skin when I sit

She runs up our stairs no more
But I hear her feet gently rising
Stairs we painted and carpeted
Painted with our palette of love
Carpeted as love is not enough

She sleeps in our bed no more
My heart is handed back to me
And it murmurs in dream states
Strikes nightly new blank slates
Chiseling tales of how were we

And the fossil, it is me, you see
The tiles are closing around me
As she chalks bright new marks
On grey, on a graphite grey day
I am stuck between grey sheets

Icicle

In the melting ice I witness,
I witness loss of frozen form,
form once elegance shaped,
shaped as frigid violence.

With each chilly drip I ache,
I ache harder than ever before,
before the spell had been broken,
broken now, once frozen fast.

Her love diminished so slowly,
so slowly, so coldly, so clearly,
clearly I watched it waning,
waning before my hollow eyes.

Here I lie prone, in thought,
in thought on the cold hard ground,
ground that surely must take me,
me shattered by the thaw.

Now let that icicle fall,
icicle fall and pierce my heart,
heart burst and spill blood red,
red blood over crystalline shards.

Binned

And I remember
Our last summer.

Me waiting for you
To grow into you
The re-birthed you
With the new hair
Adult asymmetric
With that new walk
Professional mimic
And your new talk
From lips, ceramic
So...
Not from you
Not with the heat
From the meat
Of the lover you.

I think I knew
That it was coming
That you
Were thinking
Of leaving
Me...
Of forcing me

To go grow
Another branch
And to go grow it
On another tree.

I never would have
Stopped believing
Thought of leaving
I still can't...
I can't manage
Through tears
And perhaps
Through years
As autumnal leaves
Swiftly swirling
In the chill
Of our winters grieving
I can't manage
That cleaving.

You see my essence
Gone witching
Wanders with you
And your presence
It presents

Your nose

And your eyes

And your breasts

And when in deep

We talk it through

We work things out

We start anew.

But how could you?

You left or rather

You began, renewed.

You grew a fresh limb

Which sprouted from

The tear in the bark

That gash so stark

That I left as I fell

On that fell day.

What are you now?

And who am I?

Am I he?

The one

Who waited

Patiently

For the axe

For you

To send me away

To graft to another

Perhaps...

Someday...

Or to lie

Dank and sodden

Being scratched at

Being fed upon

And glowing, rotten.

In those final weeks

I was working on us

Making captured moments

Play a slideshow,

Now a freaks sideshow

Displaying lost love.

I bought you a car

So as to free you

Gave you my gear

So that you could grow

Separately, independently

Into the mountaineer

That I helped you

To be.

And you? What about you?

Were you thinking of me?

Working for us?

Or, as I think likely

Were you thinking of you?

Planning your future?
Your future less me...

In those final days
The finality wasn't clear
I spent my time
Stupidly, like a cow
Approaching slaughter day
Wide eyed and afraid
But not of the obvious
Just of the unknown
And you took my hand
And led me to a dark space
And in that place
You shot sharp words
Into my by now
Freaking face
And I fell
And I begged
But to no avail
As for you,
It and I were dead.

And I changed
A parchment I became
That cow's skin
Pulled tight
A skin that we
Had lived in

With marks in ink
That we made on
Recording the days of
Our time, now gone.

Fourteen seasons
All you dismissed
And without reason
And I was drying out
I became crisp
And you took that chance
And crumpled me
In your now
Powerful fist
And I
I am dismissed.

And now
You don't see me.
As I am binned
And I rest inside
My metal box
No home now
For your heart is fled
And with it I shed
Life's reason
Our strength...
Your heart which
With mine

In days past
Bled out and
Our blood combined.

Of That red wine
We drank deep draughts
And I laughed with you
At the joy
In the craft
Of our love.

But now I am cowed
I am that cow
Docile and dense
Chewing the crud
Of two lives
Who camp now
In not one
But in two tents.

And I am left
No longer the lover
With bounding credence
But with a notion
With a swelling commotion
With synapses intense

I am left Incensed.

Contact Me!

Please do contact me with feedback regarding this collection of poetry.

You can get in touch by email and also at my facebook page.

I will respond to all excepting the outrageously offensive...

Please have a look at the website too - not much on there at the mo but new work will be published on a regular basis.

welshlamb@me.com

www.facebook.com/AmuseMePress

www.amusemepress.co.uk

Andy Muse

Andy is a self employed Adventure Activity provider, massage therapist and life model.

He lives in his van with his lurcher, Rowan, and parks up in Cardiff and the surrounding South Wales countryside.

His adventure business offers quality days out in Wales taking part in activities such as Mountain Biking, Gorge Walking and Coasteering. He is an outspoken provider and has worked long and hard to drive up the standard of adventure activity provision in Wales. This has invariably not made him friends.

Andy is an aromatherapist and manual lymphatic drainage specialist. He calls himself 'The Skinworker' and although he doesn't have time to bodywork as an income he does retain a few clients to help maintain his hands on healing skills.

Being the most naked person in the UK, Andy has gathered about him a team of professional Cardiff based life models, happy naked people, if you like. The dedication he has shown to professionalism in the provision of life models to colleges and to the models themselves, improving rates of pay beyond that usually achieved by life models even in London, is a positive reflection of Andy's ethics.

Andy believes in sharing wealth and building communities and this is evidenced by his work developing activity and arts networks in Wales.

In his spare time Andy travels, walks the mountains of the UK and listens avidly to two three radio stations, Radio 4, The Alex Jones Show and Coast to Coast AM.

From those shows you will gather that he is politically active, engaged and full to brimming with conspiracy facts and tales of the strange.

Andy is a remote viewer, trained by the last trainer working for Project Stargate and he has a keen interest in psychic abilities, time travel and earth mysteries.

Given the time, Andy is happiest while naked in the sun on a secluded beach in France.

Reactions To A First Reading

'You are the Quentin Tarantino of British poets' Matt Warren - Editor of 'The Lady' magazine

'Ruthlessly romantic laced with naked truths' Alexander Wharton - Poet

'Some tender love poetry' - Juke Open Mic, Cardiff

'In an instant you are gripped by the raw and honest account of life, and, of relationships. This poetry verbalises what we often shy away from verbalising, though we feel it daily and deeply. It is honest, passionate, and often uncomfortable. But it is real. And perhaps what we all need to move forwards is to be 'real' about what we feel, where we've been, and where we're going. Speaking especially as a Brit... to throw off our Britishness and cast aside our ease to offence. This is life. This is real. This needs to be expressed... read... and understood...' - Layla Welford, Cardiff Creative Writers

'Juicy, bloody, venomous stabs at the heart' - Anna Hurford, Aspiring Writer